LAW (

ATTRACTION FOR

BEGINNERS

Discover how to attract the things you

want into your life and manifest the

future you desire

CECIL DAVIDSON

Table of contents

Introduction

The beginning of a new level of comfort and awareness in your life is upon you right now. This book will alter the way you present yourself to the world, as well as the way the world presents itself to you.

Greetings and welcome to a new way of being. Consider for a second if you had infinite resources at your disposal right now. You have the ability to accomplish, have, experience, and become whatever you set your heart on. What if you were entirely supported and led by the cosmos, as if you were in the flow of things? What if you were in touch with your intuition, knowing that the next chance will present itself at any given time, and then the next one, and the next one, and the next one? The universe would take care of you, and everything would turn out precisely the way you wanted it to—because you created it in the first place. It's a possibility.

A big chance of your purchasing this book is based on the fact that you haven't yet created what you want in your life. You may be familiar with the concept of manifestation, but do you understand all of the principles and the proper sequence in which to put them into action? Are you questioning whether or not you're doing this manifestation thing correctly? Perhaps you've already achieved some success, but you're feeling a tug to pursue a more ambitious goal in your heart. Over-efforting to materialize something greater has, on the other hand, resulted in burnout and worry.

Let go of the notion of hustling or pushing in order to achieve your goals. That method is out of date and ineffective. To explain further, most people overcomplicate the manifestation process, but once you understand how it works and the actions you must do in order to enable your dreams come true, it is really pretty easy. It makes no difference if you're a beginner or a seasoned manifestor; this book will teach you a new method to accept what's in your heart and bring it into your reality. As you can see, the more you try to force things to happen, the more difficult it will be. The more your ability to open up and let in the things that you want, the simpler it will be to bring them into your life. This is exactly what I'm about to show you.

Here, you'll discover how to get out of your own way so that you may achieve your maximum personal potential. You'll be able to release limiting beliefs, find what you actually desire, and develop new habits that will allow you to experience endless richness and pleasure in your life. And, in reality, you are the only one who is preventing your goal from becoming a reality. It is up to you to decide whether or not to let whatever wants to get in. Are you ready to experience love, prosperity, health, and success in your life? What about that huge creative project you've been meaning to accomplish for a long time?

We are all naturally born manifestors, regardless of our circumstances. You have the ability to achieve anything. If you can conceive anything, you can probably make it happen. As a result of the knowledge that you are in charge of your own life, wouldn't you want to live the finest life you possibly could? This is your opportunity. This is a watershed

moment in your life. This is the beginning of your

metamorphosis.

Chapter One

How Manifestation Works

The first thing you must comprehend is how manifestation works and why you may have seen varying degrees of success in the past. When it comes to intentionally creating what you desire in your life, this fundamental knowledge is essential. Whatever our beliefs on manifestation, the reality is that we are all manifesting, whether we are aware of it or not. You are now in the process of constructing your own world. However, if you don't understand the process, you'll end up attracting all kinds of random objects to you that may or may not fit your wishes at the time of attraction. And you'll never be pleased with what comes up for you in the first place.

You can have, be, and experience everything you wish when you use conscious manifestation techniques to achieve your goals. You are a part of the co-creation of the cosmos. You'll discover all you need to know about the science of manifestation, as well as the origins of it all. You'll quickly discover that everything is made out of energy and that you are inextricably linked to the rest of the cosmos. It is possible to rely on universal laws to act in your best interests at all times. Manifestation is a lot less complicated than you would imagine. Magic happens when you are able to reconnect with the essence of who you actually are. And it all begins with your imagination and your willingness to consider the possibilities.

Consider the following for a moment: There is a reason why your dreams selected you. They want to manifest themselves via you. What if everything you've always assumed was just your imagination — pure fiction — is really you foreseeing what's going to happen in the future? So, what if you were intended to have and experience everything you've ever wished for yourself but were prevented from doing so? What would you do differently if you were in my position? How would you navigate your way across the world? How about with self-assurance, ease, and grace?

The majority of individuals don't have large enough dreams. And it is the very first manner in which they restrict themselves. Unless you have faith in your abilities, you will not be successful in your endeavors. That is all there is to it. However, if you are able to increase your capacity for what you feel is feasible for yourself, you will open the door to even more success and wealth.

How to Put it in practice.

Close your eyes and allow yourself to think that you can be, have, or do whatever you desire. Do this for a few minutes. What would you be doing with your life if you had infinite resources and were certain that the universe was on your side? What city would you be residing in? Who would you like to have in your life? For you, what would be enjoyable to develop and enjoy experiencing?

During this stage of the procedure, everything is possible. Nothing is too far out of the ordinary for you. All you're doing is utilizing your imagination to have a better knowledge of what you want. What is it that you are looking for right now? It may be different from what you had in mind when you first started looking. That's perfectly OK as well. Allow yourself to daydream about living the life of your dreams.

Use the law of attraction to your advantage.

In order to really learn how to materialize your desires, you must first get a basic understanding of the law of attraction and how it works. The law of attraction states that if you ask for something, it will be given to you. You attract things to yourself that are compatible with the energy you are putting forth. Using the analogy of a radio, you emit an energy signal and get corresponding signals from the cosmos in return. To put it another way, the law of attraction states that your ideas manifest into your reality. Whatever you think about becomes a reality. It is an unbreakable rule of nature.

As an example of a scientific rule of the universe that is commonly acknowledged as true, let's take a look at Newton's law of gravity, which is also largely regarded as true. As stated by Newton's law, any two bodies in the universe are attracted to each other by a force that is directly proportional to the product of their masses and inversely proportional to the square of their distance from one another. For better or worse, if you let this book to slip from your grasp, it will hit the ground. Although the gravitational force cannot be seen, its effects may be felt by the human body. The law of attraction is the same in all situations. It is a global rule that is just as real as the law of gravity. The fact that it is there and constantly in operation may not be visible to the naked eye, but it is.

Even if you're skeptical about how this works, give yourself permission to experiment with the concept. Allow yourself to consider the notion that your thoughts are the ones that shape your reality for a little period. Perhaps you're asking yourself, "If my ideas are creating my reality, then why am I not receiving the results I desire?" Everyone would be wealthy if it were as easy as declaring, "I'm a billionaire," and then becoming one. But that is not the case.

What you say is just a portion of the puzzle, to be sure. It is possible to see through the surface of beliefs to the deeper levels of beliefs. Those hidden layers, as is the case for many of us, are the ones that prevent you from achieving your true potential. This is because your ideas are out of sync with what you want.

Author Pam Grout, who has written the New York Times bestselling book E-Squared, guides readers through experiments that they may do on themselves to demonstrate that what we think about becomes reality. In one chapter, readers are advised to plant green bean seeds in an empty egg carton, which is a fun and creative activity. They are instructed to speak favorably to the seeds on the left side of the tray and negatively to the seeds on the right, while watering them evenly every two days with the optimistic anticipation that the seeds on the left would develop more quickly than the others. Moreover, guess what? It has been discovered time and time again that those who were spoken to favourably and who were projected to develop quicker did in fact grow faster. What do you say to yourself on a daily basis to motivate yourself?

Consider the following scenario: you're in a restaurant and you're ready to make an order for something to eat. You make the decision that you want pizza. So you inform the waiter that you would like to place an order for pizza. However, after the waiter has left, you can't stop thinking about how delicious that Kale Caesar Salad sounded in the first place. And you begin to have second thoughts about your choice to order the pizza. Plus, pizza isn't really good for you, aren't they? And you start to feel bad about yourself for having ordered it. You are under the impression that it will cause you to gain weight. You're a glutton for punishment. You should really consider going on a diet. In any case, it's not going to be that good. You approach the waitress and inform her that you would want to cancel your order. However, they had already begun to prepare the pizza. If you keep flagging down the waiter and altering your order, the chef (or, in this instance, the cosmos) will be at a loss as to what to send you next. Because you're thinking all of these ideas, whether you're conscious of them or not, you're sending conflicting signals to the cosmos. No matter what you decide to order, you must first know what you want and be confident in your choice of ingredients.

You've said that you'd want something. You repeat affirmations, which are positive phrases that confirm that you already have what you're searching for in your life. Although you feel it is doable on the outside, you are not convinced on the inside. You have your doubts about whether or not it will happen. Alternatively, you may believe that you do not really deserve it. As a result, you persuade yourself that you aren't sure whether it is what you really want. These are the kinds of ideas that we all have from time to time. I'm going to assist you in breaking out of that loop so that you may maintain a high vibration while manifesting your desires.

According to the law of attraction, you will attract things that have a frequency that is similar to the one you emit into the world. Therefore, you want your vibration to be as high as possible so that you may attract even more pleasant events into your life.

You were chosen by your aspirations. Given that you've visualized your goals, you may be certain that achieving them is within reach. All that is required is that you create a sense of possibility.

So, the next time a crazy thought creeps into your head—for example, "I want to do something outrageous"—you have a few options for how you could respond:

Close the door on all possibilities. You may say to yourself, "Oh, I'd never do anything like that," and then go on.

Allow for a flicker of hope that is immediately dashed to the sidelines. You could say to yourself, "Wow, that's a great idea!"

Cultivate an attitude of possibilities. "Wow, I'm really writing a book!" you think to yourself. "How awesome is that?" It's possible that you'll get enthused about the prospect of writing the book. Allowing yourself to think that you are genuinely becoming an author is a viable option. Assume you're the one who's authoring the book. After that,

20

picture seeing a book with your name on the cover on a shelf at your favorite bookshop.

Can you feel the differences in the way your body reacts to these two situations?

Whenever you approach problem solving from a position of fostering potential, your ideas are born from a place of trust. As a result of what is currently taking place, you are aware that you have been given the concept. When you believe in your visions, you can take action to manifest them. And after you've done that, it'll be much simpler to put your ambitions into action.

Having a new thought indicates that you are actively constructing your new reality, which means that if you are now in a "poor" mood, you have the power to alter it. There is no need to point the finger at anybody. You may simply choose to think that the situation will improve, and in doing so, you will have already had an impact on the outcome of the issue. If you believe that the situation will improve, you are actively contributing to its improvement.

In Israel's Weizmann Institute of Science, a well-known research of electrons was conducted, which shown that "the more the quantity of 'watching,' [the greater the observer's] effect on what really occurs." We are aware that an item does not exist in a vacuum, irrespective of its observer. You have an effect on the item itself by paying attention and intending to do something. To put it another way, the more conscious you are of your ideas, the more influence you will have on the result of your thoughts.

Not only do the potential for your dreams exist inside you, but the very fact that you are thinking them in the first place indicates that they already exist in the physical world. In other words, you already have what you're seeing in your mind's eyes. When you nurture potential, you put your faith in the fact that merely having an idea implies it's going to materialize. As a result, manifesting is more about letting what is already there for you to come in than than striving to force anything to emerge. It's a test of faith and openness to be received.

How to Put it in practice.

Pay close attention the next time an idea arises into your thoughts to see how you react to it. Anytime you catch yourself thinking, "I could never do that," recognize them and then make the intentional decision to behave differently.

For the time being, just substitute "I could never" or "I can't" with "How can I?" Instead of blocking off all possibilities for your aspirations, you create a place for them to manifest themselves in this manner. Opening oneself open to potential is as simple as saying to yourself, "Hmm, that's a fascinating concept." Instead of replying, "Hmm, that's a fascinating thought, but it's unlikely to happen," instead, "I wonder how that might happen?" If you foster the prospect of it happening, your dream may come true. "Where there's a will, there's always a way," is a phrase that you are surely acquainted with. After all, there is always a way. At this point, don't be worried with the how of achieving your goals and objectives. It will eventually surface. Concentrate on the what, confident in the knowledge that everything you imagine is feasible to bring to fruition.

Make a pact with the universe in order to manifest your dreams.

A "participatory universe," according to theoretical physicist John Wheeler, is one in which everyone can contribute to the understanding and prediction of the properties of a physical system. Wheeler's contribution to quantum physics, which is the branch of physics that uses quantum theory to describe and predict the properties of a physical system, was greatly influenced by this idea. Quantum theory states, in a nutshell, that everything is made up of energy and that your thought waves have an effect on particles of matter. When you anticipate a certain outcome, you are essentially encouraging that outcome to manifest

25

itself physically. In terms of manifestation, this is encouraging news. When we think about it, there is a limitless field of possibility and potentiality in the cosmos that we may impact via our ideas. Every minute of our lives, we are actively shaping our world.

We aren't merely spectators to our own existence. We're taking part in the game. Alternatively, as I choose to conceive of it, it implies that we are co-creating with the cosmos itself. This relates back to the notion that when you conceive anything, you are somewhat creating a new thought on your own, but you are also intuiting an idea that the world is sending out.

Every time you have a new concept, you are in fact forming your new reality; however, it is not simply your ideas that are building your reality; it is also your actions. You must imagine yourself in the position of having your aspirations already come true. For example, if you want to be affluent, you should engage in activities that make you feel wealthy in the present moment. Take a trip to your favorite upmarket boutique and put on items that make you feel like a million dollars. You may even purchase something for yourself to take home and wear to make yourself feel more rich in your life. By concentrating your attention on how it feels to get what you want, you send a clear message to the universe about your intentions. In addition, the cosmos is a mirror of your ideas and feelings. This message is repeated over and over again: "Yes, thank you for your order. "It has been received and delivered." In addition, if you are able to take action on the ideas that are presented to you, you will be able to bring your wishes into physical reality. Say you've been thinking about taking a specific class, and then you get an e-mail from the instructor you've been interested in learning from, offering a chance to study with him or her while attending a class that just happened to be in your area. Those are messages from the universe, guiding you on how to bring your aspirations to fruition. However, you must take an active role in the process. It is necessary for you to act on the ideas that the universe provides you. If the universe perceives that you are paying attention, it will continue to communicate with you.

You see, the fact is that you are never on your own when it comes to anything.

The concept that there is a secret network linking all of life is a part of quantum theory, according to which there is no such web. We may believe that we are distinct from the rest of the universe, yet in reality, we are all connected by a same universal field. In the event that you were to look at your atoms under a microscope, you would see that they are continually moving and vibrating. The boundaries between one object and another get more blurred as you examine even more closely. Atoms are constantly circling and spinning in their orbits around one another. Despite the fact that everything seems to be independent, it is everything interrelated. We are all contributing to the evolution of the global awareness of the planet. You can't tell where one hue stops and another starts when you're looking at us, just like a rainbow.

In a similar vein, your ideas do not just affect you; they also have an impact on others. Consider a moment when you came into a room and were greeted with a wave of overpowering bad energy. Someone you've come into touch with is emitting negative energy, and you can sense it. This phenomena does not just manifest itself on an individual level; it also manifests itself on a global scale. Major tragedies are felt across the globe, causing waves of grief or dread in the wake of them. There have also been worldwide days of peace and prayer that have been scientifically investigated for their good impact on the conduct of individuals who are in no way related to the peaceful acts taking place throughout the world. According to a Washington crime rate research, there was a 23 percent drop in crime as a result of meditation over a three-week period in Washington D.C., during which 4,000 persons focused on peace, according to the findings. The police commissioner had earlier said that the only way to decrease crime by 20% would be for there to be 20 inches of snow on the ground! And, perhaps most surprisingly, the crime rate jumped immediately after the meditation session concluded.

There is a great deal of scientific evidence to support the concept of manifestation. But how can you put it in practice in your daily life? What happens when something unexpected enters the scene and knocks you off your game? Remember that the universe is a yes universe; it is a mirror of your ideas, and it is constantly supporting you and encouraging you to walk into your greatness. So, materialize anything you desire because the universe is a yes universe. Whatever we say or believe, whether it's good or bad, the world responds affirmatively to us.

As an example, recall the last time you were having a poor day. You drop your cup of coffee. Your youngster has a temper tantrum and has to be restrained. You are late for work because you missed your train. When you get at work, you learn that you have missed an essential meeting. What gave you the impression that you had forgotten? You're caught in a downward cycle of your own making. While it may seem that a downward spiral is unavoidable, it is possible to turn the situation around. It all begins with your frame of mind. If you tell yourself, after spilling your coffee, "I'm having a poor day," you're likely to repeat the pattern of having a bad day over and over and again. Keep in mind that the universe is a mirror. It is likely that if you state that you are having a horrible day, you will get further evidence to reinforce that opinion. Instead, say something like, "Oops, I spilt my coffee," or something like. Then you should forgive yourself. Allow it to go. It is not required to set the tone for the rest of your day unless you want to let it to. You have the option to pick. So many individuals are just oblivious of their role in perpetuating this cycle of violence. However, we are living in a participatory universe.

How does manifestation truly work? It goes like this: You attract things to you depending on the vibrational frequency that you radiate out into the universe. When you're thinking positive thoughts and feeling confident, when you really believe that things are occurring for you, you'll notice that wonderful things are coming your way. This is called the law of attraction. You become aware that synchronicities are taking place. Amazing possibilities are presented to you because you are anticipating them to do so.

When you originate from a position of trust and inner knowledge, you have the ability to remain in harmony regardless of the external circumstances that arise. It is not necessary to exert effort in order to realize your ambitions. All you have to do is open the door for them and allow them to enter. Once you've decided what you want, the next step is to let the world to express itself through you in whichever way it sees fit. More like a subtle tug toward something greater than oneself, this is how it feels. There is a union between the two: the cosmos and yourself.

How to Put it in practice.

Take out your manifestation diary and split a page into three columns to better understand how you interact with the cosmos.

"What I desire from the universe" should be written at the top of the first column. "What the universe needs from me" should be written at the top of the second column. "What the cosmos and I desire jointly" should be written at the top of the third column of the worksheet.

Make a list of your goals.

You're now conscious of the fact that you're a conscious participant in the events that unfold in your life. Your beliefs are continually reshaping your reality, so be aware of this.

It is now up to you to decide whether or not you will choose to think that your dreams are already a reality. These dreams are now in the process of coming true. Your life is a canvas on which to paint. It is the most extreme manifestation of your ambitions. Your dreams come to life as a result of your actions. You are the most beautiful piece of art you have ever created.

And, like with all great artists, the creative process of manifesting begins with a decision on what you want to produce next in order to begin the manifestation process. The first step is to become crystal clear on precisely what it is that you are attempting to attract into your life. This is accomplished by the establishing of an intention.

Setting your intention is just the act of identifying what you want right now and committing to it. You can have a new want that is completely different from what you've always thought you wanted, or it might be a dream that you've had for a long time. Whatever you desire, it should always feel lighter in your stomach and more thrilling rather than heavier. That's how it feels when you get a resounding yes. Even if your desire is frightening because it is so large, it should be exhilarating to pursue it. When I deal with my clients, I often discover that they are the ones who are preventing themselves from obtaining what they want simply because they haven't allowed themselves to believe that it is possible to do so. Rather than setting an aim, they just haven't allowed themselves to think that they are capable of accomplishing it. However, you now understand that your aspirations are attainable just because you had them in the first place. As a result, the following stage is to declare your purpose.

How to Put it in practice.

Let's get started with putting this lesson into practice by writing down your intentions. Although you may have previously set goals, it is always a good idea to write them again since your intentions are continually manifesting. Furthermore, what you want before may no longer be desired. Additionally, writing your objectives again and over again strengthens your belief in them.

To begin, jot down your answers to the following questions in your manifesto journal: What do you hope to create in your life? How do you plan to manifest it?

What kind of person or thing would you want to see come up in your life?

Check to see whether your responses are consistent. It's OK if they haven't done so yet. You'll get there in the end. As you read this book, choose a goal for yourself—something tiny that you will feel good about, whatever it is, that you want to happen as a consequence of your reading. For example, what would you want to obtain out of these teachings while you are reading about manifesting would be helpful to. If you're just getting started with manifestation, this will most likely seem a little more feasible in comparison to where you are right now in your journey.

Embrace the possibility of dreaming greater than what you are currently allowing yourself to think is achievable for you. In order for your vision to come to life, you must first allow it to enter your consciousness. If you haven't even envisioned it, then you're effectively slamming the door on the prospect of it ever happening in the first place. So, make a list of your two most ridiculous goals for the rest of your life. "I am a successful painter who exhibits at the Whitney Museum of American Art," for example. In my marriage, I have found happiness with the love of my life, and we travel the globe together, creating art and giving back to communities in need via our nonprofit foundation." Feel happy about whatever it is that you put down as your goals, and you will open yourself up to new possibilities.

It's normal to be apprehensive about claiming your dream in its true form. It is impossible to make a mistake while choosing a dream. You always have the option to make a decision. If something doesn't work out the first time, you may always try something else.

You'll never be completely trapped in any circumstance. Keep in mind that the cosmos is always in motion. Every cell in our bodies is always moving and vibrating, which implies that they are constantly changing and evolving as well. Every day, the skin cells in our bodies are different from the ones that were there a week ago or a year ago; everything is always shifting. Change is the normal condition of the cosmos, therefore when you are afraid of change, you are essentially afraid of the natural state of things. As an alternative, embrace change, surround yourself with newness, and keep in mind that the things that you are experiencing right now in your life—the people you are experiencing right now, the circumstances you are experiencing right now, your surroundings, wherever you are right now, your home, and the things that fill your home—those are the things that you have allowed yourself to believe are possible for you up until this point.

As a consequence, if you allow yourself to think that other things are conceivable, you will begin to see evidence of those outcomes in the people, the circumstances, the situations, the surroundings, and the possibilities that begin to appear in your life right now. I'm going to work with you to help you realize that new dream you have for yourself. It's also OK if your dream turns out to be something completely different from what you expected. Perhaps you've always believed you wanted something, but you've just realized, "I don't think I want it at all anymore." It's quite OK to adjust your dream. Pay attention to your feelings. What does it feel like to be happy right now? What is it that you are dying to let shine through you right now?

Consider the process of establishing your own vegetable garden in your mind's eye. You sow your seeds and water them to ensure that they grow. You expose them to natural light.... You have a soft spot for them. You take care of your garden on a daily basis. You have no doubts about the fact that your plants are growing. Consider the following scenario: you've planted potatoes. In addition, the potatoes are beginning to develop well under the surface of the soil. You are unable to view them. However, you are aware that they are expanding. You're pleased to see that they're expanding. The potato plant is not pulled out just as it is beginning to sprout underground and asked, "Why aren't you growing faster?" This is a common misconception.

No, you have trust in the whole course of things. You keep up the good work of watering and caring for your plants. Then there will come a day when your potatoes are finally ready to be harvested.

You would have destroyed your potatoes if you had taken them out too soon after planting them. You would have thrown a wrench into the natural cycle that was taking on under the surface. If you had given up after just a month of caring for your plant, you would never have had the opportunity to reap the benefits of the crop. So many individuals lose up on their aspirations much too early in their lives. They come across "proof" that they are not destined to actualize their aspirations at some point along the journey. However, most of the time, such proof only points to a roadblock or a limiting mindset rather than a solution. Plants continue to sprout and blossom each spring, even in the midst of the most severe winters. In the event that you're currently in the middle of a storm, remember that there's sunlight just around the corner. Even when the sun is briefly obscured by clouds, the sun is still visible.

When it comes to manifesting, I like to utilize the garden analogy since there is a gestation time during which you have to trust the process. In situations when things don't seem to be moving at a quick enough pace, it's quite acceptable to get agitated. Whenever anything like this occurs, keep the garden in mind. Instead of being dissatisfied with the absence of proof in your immediate environment, believe that you are being supported.

Even if you can't see it, remember that everything is conspiring in your favor to make things better. You may be certain that you are on the correct course.

I really like looking for evidence that I'm on the correct track. On clocks and homes, I often notice the same digits repeated over and over again. That they are angel numbers, with a special message for you, according to some, are angel numbers. They are, in my opinion, little nudges from the cosmos, indicating that I am on the correct track. Symbols such as pennies, feathers, and recurring symbols are seen as signals by some. Because I'm paying attention, I'm always aware of their presence. Each indication that emerges for you should be celebrated. Continue your journey. Continue to have confidence. Focus is the most important factor in attracting what you want into your life. As a result, keep your eyes on the prize.

- You're up to the task.

- Your fantasies are becoming a reality.

- It is happening.

- You have already begun to live the life of your dreams.

- Your life is a canvas on which to paint.

- It is the most extreme manifestation of your ambitions.

- Your dreams come to life as a result of your actions.

- Your dreams are looking to be nourished.

How to Put it in practice.

Manifesting begins in the same way that every great garden does: by determining what you want to harvest next and how you want to harvest it. You may also reverse engineer the process after you've determined what it is that you wish to manifest.

Create an image in your mind of how you'll feel after your dreams have come true in their entirety. If you start from the other end of the spectrum—from the finish line, feeding into the sensation of already having what you desire—it becomes much easier to believe that you will eventually get there, and you will.

To begin, let's look at the final product.

Ask the universe for a sign that you're on the right road after you've thought about what you want to create and are feeling your desire. It's just as straightforward as that. Alternatively, you might write it down in your manifestation diary or ask it aloud. Then make a note of any signals or synchronicities that occur during the course of your day. You will notice that the more you pay attention to the things that come up in your life, the more things will arise that will assist you in manifesting your desires.

You can envision what it would be like to be already living your dream, just as the gardener may picture the lovely dinner she will prepare with the potatoes she planted. You can imagine what it will be like to already be living your ideal. You may be certain that your garden is flourishing.

So, you're aware that manifesting begins with a burning desire and a firm confidence in your vision for the future. However, the most important ingredient that is often overlooked in conversations about the manifestation process is anticipation. Having high expectations is quite helpful when it comes to making manifestation a breeze. As you can see, Manifestation is made up of three components: desire, belief, and expectation. In other words, manifestation is the sum total of your goal, your persistent thoughts, and what you anticipate to appear for you in the real world.

You should not be concerned if your aspirations seem too far away and you do not yet have the confidence to believe in yourself. Affirmations may help you achieve this goal. They aid you in increasing your belief and expectancy, and they are a strong tool for bringing you to the point of knowing that the things you want are on their way to you.

Dr. Bruce Lipton demonstrates in his book The Biology of Belief that biology is predicated on the concept of belief. If you feel you are overweight and unhealthy, that is exactly what you will become. In addition, the inverse is true. If you sincerely think that you are healthy and strong, you will be healthy and strong as well. Genetics and DNA, according to Dr. Lipton, are not in reality the controlling factors in human biology; rather, you are in command of your own existence. The energy of your thoughts has been shown to have an effect on your DNA, according to recent research. Cells make up our whole body, which has trillions. Each cell has receptors that detect frequencies formed by your thoughts and perceptions, which are picked up by the cell.

The placebo effect, on the other hand, is something you're definitely acquainted with. Two separate groups of individuals, for example, may be given the identical drug in order to cure themselves. However, one group's pill does not contain any medication, but the other group's tablet does. The fascinating part is that, after several tests, it has been shown that groups taking the bogus pill heal at a similar rate to the control group. This is due to the fact that they think their medications are genuine. They are hopeful that they will be able to recover.

As you can see, you may anticipate positive outcomes. As a result, you might anticipate your aspirations to become a reality.

How to Put it in practice.

You must put your attention on the positive in order to anticipate that nice things will occur for you. So, get out your manifestation diary and jot down the response to the following question: "What's fresh and excellent and happening in my life right now?"

If you have a new customer, for example, you may jot down the following:

- Last night, my hubby prepared an absolutely delicious meal for me.

- The birthday gift that arrived earlier than expected

- We had just scheduled a vacation to another country.

To begin, make a list of at least fifteen items, and then continue. Typically, as you begin writing, you begin to recall other events that may have been trivial at the time of writing. You begin to see that there are many positive things to be thankful for in your life. As a result, you begin to anticipate more wonderful things to come your way. This is a workout that I like doing on a daily basis.

You may do it once a week, once a month, or as many times as you like during the year. Knowing you're going to do it again instills a sense of optimism that more nice things are on their way.

Gratitude should be practiced.

For the most part, the more appreciative you are and the more time you devote to appreciating your life, the more life will provide you with things to be thankful for. You've most likely heard of this notion before, but have you ever put it into action yourself?

It is the good energy that you expend when you are thankful that helps to attract additional things into your life for which you may be grateful. The University of California discovered that those who practiced thankfulness on a daily basis had stronger immune systems, reduced blood pressure, were more positive, cheerful, and optimistic, and felt linked to a wider world after conducting a three-year research.

While you may not always be able to control your external circumstances, you can always control your response to them. You have the freedom to pick what you want to put your energy towards in your life. You may begin to filter out the negative in your life and shine a light on all of the wonderful things that are happening as a result of practicing appreciation. In addition, when you intentionally count your blessings, you begin to notice all of the wonderful things that happen in your life.. That is how thankfulness grows and develops. It's almost as if your mind has a focus lens that hunts for and magnifies the positive aspects of life.

If you're going through a bad time right now and you're having trouble coming up with even one item to be thankful for, remember that even the little things matter. Be thankful for the following:

- The one who opened the door for you

- The person who rang up your items at the grocery store.

- The fact that you have a roof over your head (wherever it may be).

- Being given the wonderful chance to live in this world because of your parents or whomever reared you

- The food that you consumed.

- The farmers who assisted in the harvesting of your food.

- Everything you just took in, plus more

When you are able to see how much help you are receiving right now—even if you do not yet have all you desire—you are able to renew your confidence in the universe, knowing that you will always be supported no matter what. You also improve your capacity to bring your aspirations to fruition.

How to Put it in practice.

Take out your manifestation diary every night before you go to bed and jot down three things for which you are thankful. The simple act of doing so will make a significant impact in your life. It's possible that you'll want to jot down even more items than you originally planned. And that's fantastic! Continue your journey. You'll have much to write about before you know it! I have a tendency to write pages and pages of appreciation. Keep an eye on how your thankfulness grows.

Pay Close Attention to Your Tone of Voice.

It is quite simple to get engrossed on the bad without even noticing that you are doing so. However, all that is required to shift your negative mental chatter is for you to change your vocabulary in order to intentionally generate what you want in your life. Make an effort to be more deliberate with the words you use in reference to your aspirations.

Pay attention to your ideas when they are negative in nature. For example, you may be required to work a day job that you despise while you are establishing your side company. Perhaps you'll be overheard stating, "I have to go into work." As a result, you are filled with dread. Make an effort to redirect your focus away from the phrases "I have to" and toward the words "I am getting." There is always something positive hiding underneath something you despise. It's simply that you haven't searched for it. For example, you may remark, "I get to work with folks that I like spending time with."

"I get to spend an hour on the train to work reading a book and listening to my favorite music,"

In exchange for this, "I get to adorn my desk with images of individuals I care about."

As a result, concentrate on what you get to accomplish rather than what you have to do. Soon, you'll begin to realize that greater chances are beginning to present themselves to you.

Now, there are certain occasions in which altering up your language may seem a bit more difficult, but there are methods to ensure that you are still bringing pleasure into your life. For example, many individuals say things

In our yes-dominated environment, if you say those things—even if it's only to yourself—you're declaring that you don't have the time or the financial means to accomplish anything. As a result, incredible chances will present themselves, such as a fantastic vacation, and you will be unable to take advantage of them due to a lack of time or money. But that's exactly what you requested! Things will come up that you can't afford and you will have to deal with them. You're also putting your aspirations on wait until you've had more time or more money, much like when you say "When we have more money." And they will continue to exist indefinitely in the future.

When you genuinely can't afford something, it might be strange to reverse the sentence and say, "I can afford it." Instead, I propose stating, "How can I?" or something like. In this approach, you are allowing for the potential of anything rather than cutting it off totally. It's the equivalent of stating, "I'm willing to assist." Please direct me in the right direction. "I'm prepared to take a look at what could be possible."

Words have tremendous power. It's possible that you'll find yourself repeating similar sentences over and over again. "I don't have enough time," was one of my pet peeves in the past. So, can you guess what it was that I kept drawing in? Things to complete on my to-do list. If you're continuously telling yourself, "I'm so busy," it's time to get a life. "I don't have enough time," you'll be precisely what you say you'll be: occupied. You won't have time to do the activities that you like doing in your spare time.

How to Put it in practice.

Check to see if there are any phrases you use on a regular basis that you'd want to change to something more positive, and write them down in your manifestation diary. Then strike them out and create a fresh term that allows you to consider the potential of achieving your goals. Keep in mind that you have complete power over your emotions. And one of the most straightforward ways to bring about change is via your words. Don't get down on yourself every time you hear a nasty sentence come out of your mouth. This activity is just about being more aware of the language you're using in order to pick more positive-feeling phrases and ideas in the

future.

Chapter Two

Increase the scope of your perception

Now that you have a better understanding of how manifestation works, it's time to broaden your vision. The majority of individuals don't have large enough dreams. Their efforts come to an end at a certain time because they believe they can only accomplish a particular level of achievement. However, I'd want to take your goal a few notches further by tying it to a larger purpose of the United Nations. Once you've accomplished this, you may return to your present position and then take larger steps back up to the top.

Since a result, manifesting in this manner is much simpler, as you already know where you're heading and can get there more quickly. The next sections will teach you how to clarify your vision, which dream to concentrate on first, a procedure for dream growth, and diary exercises to help you write down your affirmations in the most efficient manner. You'll also discover how to elevate your energy to match the frequency of the things you want, how to comprehend what your dreams and aspirations say about you, and how to employ visualization to achieve your goals and objectives. So, if you're ready to take your dream to the next level by allowing in even more awesomeness, keep reading!

Make a definite decision about what you want.

In order to get what you want, it is necessary to first determine what it is that you wish to obtain. Please understand that you are not need to know how you will get there; you are just required to know what you are attempting to achieve instead. Once you've established that, the world will provide you with whatever you need to bring your idea to fruition!

We all have friends that want to see it first before they believe it, which is understandable. I'm sure you've heard the phrase, "I'll believe you when I see it." That is diametrically opposed to how manifestation works. Those individuals believe they will be able to identify what they want when it is shown to them. That said, they are the individuals who report being the most dissatisfied with their life. They'll never be totally happy since they haven't taken the time to figure out what happiness means to them in the first place. They aren't quite sure what they want yet. You're looking for clarification.

Are you unsure of how to get the clarity you require?

Take a moment to shut your eyes and imagine that you had unlimited access to all of the money and resources in the universe at your disposal. Don't let your present status or circumstances get in the way of your goals. Consider yourself to be completely supported. Consider the following questions:

- What would your life look like if you didn't have a job?

- What do you think you'd be doing?

- What would you be doing?

- Who would you choose to spend time with?

- What would it be like to go through something like this?

There are no bad answers in this game. Usually, the initial pictures or concepts that appear in your mind are the result of your intuition—your inner desire—speaking out for itself. To let your imagination to go wild, close your eyes and close your eyes. Accept it and move forward.

Think about the one item in your life that, if you were able to do it, would make the most impact in your life starting from this point. Make an attempt to visualize what you're talking about.

Obviously, there is a great deal that we want to materialize in our life, and I am often asked, "What should I concentrate on first?" Consider concentrating on the one item that will have the greatest impact and that will have a rippling effect on everything else. What exactly would be that one thing? I want you to put down the one thing that will make the most impact in your life and will alter everything for you as soon as you realize what it is. This is what you are hoping to develop in the near future. If you are aiming to produce something monumental, it is likely that this is not the case.

How to Put it in practice.

In order to materialize your desires, you must first have clarity about what you want. This is the basis for achieving your goals and manifesting your wishes. Make clarity a part of your daily routine to assist you in determining what you really want to bring into existence. Make a pot of tea by boiling water. Make yourself a cup of coffee or a cup of hot chocolate. Light a candle, get into a comfortable chair with your favorite beverage, and begin writing.

Close your eyes and go through the visualization technique that was detailed in the preceding section once again. Consider the possibilities! Don't allow the passage of time or your current location stand in the way of your goals. To be more specific, the more absurd the better. After you've envisioned, write down where you want to be in each of the following eight areas of your life:

- Home Health Love

- Friends/community   Career/creative Financial

- Travel Spirituality

Now it's time to go specific. The universe is a fan of specifics. Describe your current residence. What is the address of your residence? What does it seem to be like? Is your bedroom painted a certain color, and what kind of bed do you sleep in? How does it feel to be a resident there?

When you wake up in the morning, what is your first impression? What do you hear outside your window, and what do you eat for breakfast, are all important questions. I'm curious in how much money you earn in a year. How much money do you have in your savings account and in your wallet, and so on. Have you gotten the picture? It is preferable to explain your dreams in as much detail as possible in order to be able to genuinely experience them.

And, perhaps most crucially, Use the present tense while writing. Instead of stating "I want to attract my perfect life mate," you may say "I am happily married to the love of my life," which would be more accurate. Take pleasure in the experience, even if it seems strange at first. This is a lighthearted activity. The more enjoyment you take in your work, the greater results you will notice. Trust me on this.

Don't be concerned if you're still a little stumped. Fill in the blanks of the following questions in your manifestation notebook for even more clarity:

- What do you like doing the most?

It's possible that they are insignificant. They are, however, hints as to what you are really passionate about. That might pave the way for a more expansive vision. (For example, I like being outdoors in nature.)

- What do you want to gain knowledge about?

To learn how to construct a website, for example, has long been a dream of some people.

If yes, is there an issue in the world that you would want to see resolved? Consider what it is that is upsetting you and how you would want to be a part of finding a solution to that problem.

Pay attention to your feelings. What is it that has been speaking to you for a long period of time? You may be experiencing feelings of longing that you haven't been able to express because you've been frightened to. Are there recurring dreams, indications, or synchronicities that you're experiencing? Pay attention to the pull that is coming from inside, rather than what other people have told you that you should do in the past. They may or might not be a good fit. It is entirely up to you to decide.

Using a new page in your diary, make a list of everything you know you don't want to include in your journal after you've answered these questions. For example, you may have determined that you do not desire a certain style of relationship or employer since your previous experiences with them were unsuccessful. This is really beneficial because, once you know what you don't want, you can develop statements that are diametrically opposed to what you do want. After you've completed, go through what you wrote for what you don't want and write down the polar opposite for each sentence you came up with before. Finally, rephrase what you want using the present tense for each sentence in order to achieve your goal.

Make Use of Your Past to Create Positivity.

Keep in mind all of the things you've previously accomplished in your life whenever you're feeling unsure or discouraged about achieving your big objective. Positive proof from your past, or PPP, is a term I use to describe this kind of evidence.

It's a terrific tool to have on hand when you're having one of those days when your self-doubt creeps in and you feel like giving up since you've been working and aren't seeing any results. Even if you're a master manifestor, those self-concerns will still arise, but PPP will assist you in eliminating those doubts.

Try to think of anything amazing that you've done in your life thus far. It might be something significant in your life that you are really proud of. For example:

• Moving out on your own and into that apartment are both big steps.

- Applying to and being accepted into a university

- Marketing your company's products and services successfully.

- Getting complimentary tickets to your favorite concert or a backstage pass to meet your favorite star after watching a play on Broadway are just a few examples of what you may expect.

- You're going through the process of having a kid.

You accomplished your goal! It's very great. You are really strong. If you're capable of these incredible feats, you're capable of anything. It all comes down to having a positive attitude and manifesting from that position. Things have materialized in your life as a result of your efforts.

Whatever the situation, there's always something to look back on.

How to Put it in practice.

Make a note of all of the things you've been able to materialize thus far in your life and keep it in your manifestation diary. They should be significant events that cause you to beam with pride when you think about them. Make a start right away, and then go back to this list if you have any uncertainties. "Wow, I was able to materialize all of those things!" you could think.

That one item that you're clinging onto that seems so important no longer seems so important because you recall that the self-doubt and dread that you were experiencing with all of the other things was also present. However, you were able to get beyond your fears, take action, and actualize your desires. As a result, you are free to pursue your interests.

Make a list of your affirmations.

Later in this chapter, you set out your goals for the rest of your life and became more detailed about what you wanted to achieve in each aspect of your life. And now that you've written down your aspirations, it's time to create affirmations that are based on what you've imagined. Affirmations are what they sound like. They are brief, affirmative statements that serve to ground your vision. The remark will be more compelling if it is kept to a minimum of words. As an example, I am a successful company owner.

- I possess a lovely white cottage on the ocean that I like spending time in.

- I am surrounded by the most lovely and supportive people.

- My work is truly cherished and appreciated by those who know and care about me.

- Money pours into my bank account like a torrent.

Affirmations assist you in getting to a state of positive thinking and believing that good things are on their way to you. Your brain may be retrained and your thinking pattern can be altered by repeatedly repeating affirmations.

When compared to what you wrote earlier, how are affirmations different? You must persuade yourself that you already have the things you are attempting to materialize in order to succeed. Affirmations may be said aloud if desired. However, even putting them down might assist you in claiming your objectives. In other words, it's going one step farther than merely setting an objective. You're asserting that you already have what you desire in your life. You're doing far more than just placing your order in the cosmos.

You're bringing it to life.

Once you've written your affirmations down, you may repeat them on a regular basis to help you achieve your goals. This is something you can do on your own, or you can use them to produce an affirmation video (which I'll cover later in this chapter). Even if you only write your affirmations down and then forget about them, it is plenty. Putting your aspirations down on paper is the first step toward realizing them.

How to Put it in practice.

Remove your manifestation diary from your bag and open it to the section where you put down what you desired in each of the following aspects of your life:

- Home Health Care Is a Pleasure

- Friends/community

- Career/creative   Financial   Travel Spirituality

After you have written your visions, write two or three brief, concise affirmations for each area using the following guidelines:

Use the present tense to express yourself. If you want to be a millionaire, say "I am a millionaire," not "I will be a billionaire" or "I want to be a millionaire."

Positive statements should be used. The cosmos is incapable of comprehending negatives or "do nots." It just hears the main point of the conversation. Whenever you wish to avoid anything, use a positive language to express the polar opposite of what you want to avoid. In the example above, if you declare, "I am debt-free," the universe will only hear the word "debt." Instead, say something along the lines of "I am financially independent." Alternatively, you may state "My back is strong and healthy" instead of "I have no back discomfort." What started out as "I want to shed 10 pounds" has evolved into "My body is healthy and fit." I am a size 6 female. I'm in such good shape! I go to the gym every day. The meals I consume make me aware of what I'm putting into my body, and I feel good about my decisions."

Make a point of being explicit. Read those two versions of the same aim aloud and pay attention to the differences that you detect when you read them both. The more exact you are in your description, the more likely it is that you will be able to genuinely experience your vision. The purpose of writing affirmations is to help you achieve your goals.

Make your story credible. If you don't really believe the affirmation, you won't feel good about yourself, and the affirmation will not be effective. So, strive for the stars and get enthused about the possibilities, but make sure you trust what you're seeing. It's possible that you're more comfortable expressing something like "I earn at least $150,000 a year" or "I make six figures a year from my company" rather than "I'm a billionaire." Despite the fact that it should be a stretch, it must be plausible.

Add thankfulness remarks at the conclusion of all of your affirmations to make them more meaningful. "I earn six figures a year from my company," for example, may be followed with the phrase "I am thankful for the abundance of money that comes to me from every direction."

Include details about your charitable contributions. For example, "I utilize my ability to make a difference in the world, and I am proud of the job that I do." "I am proud of the work that I do."

Add a "I forgive myself" statement to your affirmations once you've completed this process. It's possible that you're being much too critical of yourself when it comes to what's showing up for you. Consequently, writing "I forgive myself" dissolves any bad thoughts you may have against yourself that are rooted in your previous experiences. You may also forgive other persons who have crossed your path in life. Especially beneficial if you're trying to cling on to something that you know you should let go of, such as a broken relationship or a job loss. It is vital to understand that when you employ forgiveness phrases in affirmations, you are not need to explain why you are doing so. If you declare your reasons for doing something, your subconscious mind interprets your reasons as an affirmation, and you will become more focused on attracting more of that to you. So, instead of saying, "I forgive you, Michael, for hurting me," you might say, "I forgive you, Michael," or something like. The same rule applies to you as it does to everyone else.

Concentrate on achieving your big dream.

We had a short discussion about your major ambition in the "Set Your Intention" section of Part 1 of this series. Is there anything you want to do that would make the largest impact in your life if you were able to do it? Yes, you will materialize whatever you have written down, but we want to start with your most essential dream and direct your energy there first, before moving on to the others.

Keep in mind that you have already manifested a great deal in your life. I'm assuming you completed the practice in which you wrote down your prior incarnations. This dream should be your most ambitious vision to date. If you're here to build anything, make the most of your time here. Because after all, why not live the most fulfilling life you can possibly envision for yourself?

Instead than focusing on manifesting any little ambition, focus on setting the most outlandish goal for your life. Allow oneself to be open to a fresh vision. When you speak about your great dream, you get a glimmer of excitement in your eyes. It's the life you've always wanted. It's something that, if you could do it, be it, or have it, you'd be on top of the world, and you would be. It has the effect of making you feel lighter. It's so enormous that it's difficult to comprehend the scale of it. When you think about what your life might be like if your wish came true, you become a little afraid. You, on the other hand, want it. You're adamant on having it.

You've been deliberating about it for some time now. You're not sure when or how it will happen, but you know it will. It has to happen. It's something your heart longs for. It's the reason you're reading this book in the first place. Have you grasped the concept? Then it's time to put your plans into action.

How to Put it in practice.

Once you've decided on your big desire, I want you to write it down in your manifestation diary to keep track of it. This is a safe zone, so please feel free to elaborate on what you stated in Part 1 when you established your purpose. Don't be afraid to express yourself. Make a point of being explicit. Make a list of everything. Write in the present tense, as though you already had the item in your possession. For example, instead of writing an affirmation, you're writing a paragraph on what it's like to be living your goal. Keep in mind to concentrate just on your most ambitious goal. The objectives you set for yourself in all of your other areas of life will contribute to the realization of this vision. You are not required to rewrite any of those complimentary dreams in this case, though. Simply go into further depth on the one major point. It is not necessary to write a book. Simply define what you're writing about and see what happens as you write.

Do you have butterflies in your stomach? Simply choose your most ambitious goal and give yourself permission to pursue it. There is no such thing as a bad choice. Once you've realized your first goal, you can always change your mind about it. As long as you are alive, you will have new wants that will manifest themselves. That is very typical! What it means to be a master manifestor includes all of the things listed above. All that counts is that you be detailed in your description of your dream or the emotion that you are experiencing.

Visualize the Reality of Your Dream.

When it comes to manifesting, visualizing is one of the most crucial skills you can do. When you fully experience your dream with all of your senses, your subconscious is tricked into thinking that your dream has already occurred. You will notice a significant improvement in your life when you do this!

Instead of just sitting in meditation and visualizing what you want to happen, which is a fantastic technique, visualizing should include physically embodying your desire and experiencing it from a vibratory standpoint. Our visualizations are done so that when we feel the energy of what we desire, we may attract things to ourselves that are of the same vibration. This is an example of the law of attraction in action. In other words, the purpose of visualization is to experience what it would be like to already own the object of your desire. This will help you attract whatever it is that you want.

Is it true that visualizing is effective?

Sometimes our dream is something we feel we are unable to walk into because it is so large and overwhelming. It might be anything from a new house or vehicle to an ideal romantic partnership or anything else we've never experienced before. That's OK with me. Allow yourself to envision and experience what it would be like to have it right now, no matter how far away it seems to be.

Test-drive the vehicle of your choice. Go on an excellent date to a fantastic restaurant with your significant other! Make more room in your house, feel more enriched in your surroundings, and practice more self-care. Find something that will make you feel wonderful right now, and do it immediately. In order to effectively use visualization, you must first allow yourself to feel the way you want to feel even if you do not yet have that object or achieve the outcome you wish.

How to Put it in practice.

So, what method do you use to visualize? Constructing a vision board and repeating affirmations are excellent first steps. However, they barely scrape the surface of the art of visioning. Make use of the affirmations you prepared in the "Write Your Affirmations" section of this chapter as a guidance throughout the visioning phase.

Step into your vision with your heart and allow it to be experienced through all of your senses to begin.

Close your eyes and pretend that you already have everything you wish in your life. Consider the following scenario: you are invited to a party in your honor. Who else is in the room with you? What occasion are you commemorating? What are your whereabouts? What does it seem to be like? Is there any food available? What does it smell and taste like, and how does it make you feel? What do you think others are saying to you? What exactly are you up to? What are your thoughts? Take it all in with a smile, as if it were a movie playing out in your head. Take pleasure in the envisioning process. You'll get the impression that you're already living your dream.

Make a living doing what you like.

The more you remain in your heart, the simpler it will be to create your desires and goals. What exactly does this mean? Well, while you are in a pleasant state of mind, your vibrational frequency is increased. And this allows you to attract things that have a greater frequency of attraction.

What is the quickest and most effective strategy to ensure that you remain in your heart? Doing activities that you really like! As long as you are engaged in activities that you like, you will be irresistible to the things that you want to materialize in your life. Most of the time, if we examine the reasons for wanting to materialize something, we find that it is because it will enable us to feel a certain way. So, even though you don't currently have what you desire, if you can embody the emotion that goes along with it, you will be able to materialize it more rapidly.

"How can I be feeling that way right now?" you may wonder. When you pose that question, you are opening yourself up to the potential of anything happening. Perhaps you want to feel cheerful or free, so you turn on some music and start dancing around the room. Perhaps you'd want to experience more happiness in your life. So you engage in an activity that provides you delight. It might be anything as simple as going to your favorite dancing class or going to see a movie. There is something that everyone of us enjoys doing and that makes us feel pretty good about ourselves. Start doing more of the things that make you happy since, as previously said, this will alter your vibration and assist you in attracting the greater things that you want to manifest into your life. Why?

It may seem like doing what you enjoy has nothing to do with your major desire. However, everything is interconnected. A happy you increases your chances of manifesting your dreams and goals in life. Because you are vibrating at a higher frequency than happy, you are a vibrational match for your aspirations. Was it ever brought to your attention that Richard Branson's number one aim every day is to have fun? That he's one of the world's wealthiest and most successful company owners, investors, and philanthropists shouldn't come as a surprise.

Keep returning to your magical kid, who is the wellspring of all of your creative energy, if you're having difficulties figuring out what lights you up. As I've seen my daughter develop, I've observed that she has a contagious grin that she wears throughout the day. Everything was a game to her, especially when she was a baby. Take advantage of the youthful exuberance of this youngster. Take a trip to that realm of wonder and delight and see what you may find there! What do you think would be enjoyable for you to do right now? If you're having trouble coming up with ideas, I propose spending some time in nature. It always has the effect of raising your vibe. Every day you perform something you like, you will discover that the appropriate people and the perfect circumstances will appear to assist you. Amazing synchronicities begin to emerge, and you may be able to follow your intuition on some exciting journeys of discovery. Everything in your life will become an opportunity once you start doing what you love and living in this spirit.

How to Put it in practice.

Take the time today to accomplish something that you really like doing. That's all there is to it! This might be:

- Anything from going to your favorite yoga class to doing some yard work.

- Taking yourself out to supper at your favorite restaurant is a nice treat.

- While you're watching your favorite movie.

- You're out on your bike.

- Taking a bath with bubbles while holding candles.

- Getting your feet done.

- Getting a massage is a relaxing experience. Making art is something I like doing.

- Having a good time.

There shouldn't be any emotions of guilt associated with it; instead, it should make you really joyful, contented, and satisfied. Nothing except happiness.

Synchronicities.

There is a lot of promise in synchronicities. If you're paying attention, you could discover minor synchronicities in your life, or you might observe synchronicities that are so massive that they actually take your breath away. In fact, the more you pay attention to the minor synchronicities, the more and more major and significant happenings will surface to demonstrate that you are headed in the correct way. Sometimes the synchronicity is guiding you in the direction of a certain opportunity that necessitates your participation. Sometimes it's just a confirmation that you're in the midst of a manifestation maelstrom. Vortex is a phrase invented by Abraham-Hicks, master teacher of the Law of Attraction, to describe the state of being in connection with source energy—the location where all creation takes place. It implies that you are completely aligned with your aspirations while you are in the vortex of manifestation. They are beginning to materialize. Everything is turning out just how you had hoped it would. Everything has a connection to everything else. If we have an open mind and pay attention to the synchronicities, the universe will always organize the most amazing moments for us.

How to Put it in practice.

Take out your manifestation diary and jot down all of the synchronicities that you encountered during the course of your day. The more you pay attention to what is going on in your environment, the more connected you will be to the universe, and the simpler it will be to materialize your desires. If you commit to doing this for a week, you will see a difference. If you do it for a month, it will become second nature.

Starting now, as you go through this book, begin keeping a notebook of all the signals and synchronicities that occur in your life on a daily basis. It's best to do this at the end of each day or as soon as you become aware of them. Your awareness of the good indications in your environment will increase as your awareness of how much help you are receiving from the universe grows.

Chapter Three

Taking Action

Part of the effectiveness of the tactics we've explored so far is that they prepare your mind to take the action necessary to get things going in the right direction. Even while visualization, positive affirmations, and synchronicities are very beneficial, you cannot spend your whole day imagining or uttering positive affirmations in hopes of manifesting your desires or attracting your desires. You must take immediate action in order to achieve your goals and aspirations.

If you're not sure what you can do to bring your huge idea to fruition, start with something modest and incremental. Bring up the restaurant comparison from earlier in the book once again, shall we? Consider the following scenario: you're in a restaurant. Your preferred item appears on the menu, so you place an order for that particular item. However, the waiter appears and informs you of a new special that sounds really fantastic. Consider ordering it, but you are apprehensive since you are unsure if it will be as excellent as the food you are familiar with and have previously enjoyed. Choose between being safe and ordering the same thing and taking a chance on the special, knowing that it will be good.

I understand if you are the kind of person who orders the same item time and time again. If you are, you are content with what you are experiencing right now as well as the consequences of your efforts. "I'm not feeling comfortable," you could think. It is not my relationship, nor is it my house, nor is it my career that I am content with." The comfort comes from the fact that this is what you've allowed yourself to think is feasible for you up to this point in time. Moreover, the possibility of reinventing oneself and achieving greater heights exists right now. Being willing to go outside of your comfort zone is the only way to really experience something new. Instead of taking the risk, you play it safe and fall back into your comfort zone since that's all you know how to do. If you want to build and extend your business, you must purchase the promotional item!

You'll learn how to take action in this section, and you'll discover just how tasty the special truly is. Hopefully, you've spent some time practicing visualization techniques, as detailed in Part 2 of this series. It is my invitation to take a look at that area again and spend some time picturing what you want. It's time to start "behaving as if," if you've already done that.

When you behave as if you are someone else, you are creating the surroundings of the person you are impersonating. This isn't the same as "faking it till you make it," which is a common adage. Rather, it is about embracing the sensations associated with your dream. After all, if you don't trust in your own ability to actualize your dreams, no one else will.

Even if you don't completely believe it on the inside, your outer actions will assist you in getting there. For want of a better expression, your external acts may aid you in modifying your inner sentiments or beliefs. For example, when you're joyful, you'll likely grin at someone. However, it may also be used in the other direction. If you smile, you will experience happiness. Acting as though one must first smile in order to feel better is a kind of deception. Consider the implications of this. Never had a new haircut or an entirely new outfit, and then noticed that you were acting in a completely different way right away? You were undoubtedly more self-assured after that, didn't you? The way you feel changes when you act like if. If you can feel the way you want to feel right now, you'll be able to attract additional experiences that will aid in the creation of that sensation. Consider what it is that you want to become more of in your life and write it down.

Make a formal declaration. Put yourself in a position to attract what you want. It's really that simple. If pretending to be someone else is difficult, remember that you are deserving. You have earned the right to live the life of your dreams. You have the ability to be that person right now. Except for yourself, there is nothing that can stand in your way. So put on your best clothes and go out. Make decisions that your ideal self would make. Have a good time and act the role!

How to Put it in practice.

Take a moment to reflect on the huge dream you put down in your manifestation diary in Part 2 of this series. Consider what it is that you want to become more of in your life and then ask yourself that question. Consider the following scenario: you want to be a successful filmmaker. Now, in order to assist you in assuming that position, I'd like to provide you with a fun challenge:

Make an effort to dress up as the dream you and visit a location where the dream you would congregate. For example, if you have a hot physique in your dreams, you may want to treat yourself to a membership at an elite gym and enroll in one of their programs. They most likely offer a free trial week available. If you have a desire of becoming a successful filmmaker, you may want to attend a film screening at a local film festival to fulfill your ambition. Perhaps exquisite dining experiences will be a regular occurrence in your dream existence. So why not indulge in one right now? Put on your best clothes and go to the most exclusive restaurant in your neighborhood. See what it's like to eat at a posh restaurant with rich patrons. You could merely be ordering a drink, but you'll be in excellent company regardless of what you choose. You are not need to pay any money in order to complete this assignment. You may just go hang out in a different section of town where you consider yourself to be a resident. Alternatively, you may contact a real-estate professional to arrange several viewings of potential ideal houses for you. A convertible may be tested-driven at a vehicle dealership to get an idea of how it feels to drive about in one of them. Those suggestions will not cost you a thing, and you can begin behaving as if you actually do have the financial means to make these decisions right now. When you are in your dreams, you will have a better understanding of how it feels when you are not there. In addition, your body will retain a record of your encounters. In fact, you'll discover that taking care of some of these tasks for yourself may be really powerful.

Why? Because if you behave like if, you will begin to notice that the people around you are responding to your vibe and will begin to see you as the person you wish to be. And that self-reflection serves to strengthen your own conviction.

Dare to Take the Next Step in Realizing Your Big Dream.

In order to make your goals a reality, you must first choose which ones are most important. That is all there is to it. Your dream will always be on the back burner if you continue to put it off until a better time. Instead, reverse your to-do list and prioritize your major desire at the top of the list. That way, there's no getting around it. To assist bring your big idea ahead, you may take modest action actions on a regular basis.

How to Put it in practice.

Fill up the blanks of your manifestation diary with a to-do list for the day that has just three items. Do this every day. You should focus on those three items as the most important measures you can take to bring your greatest desire ahead.

Things like "do the laundry" and other tasks that may be checked off are out of the question. You would feel better about yourself if you performed three things that were terrifying to do at the same time, but you did them nonetheless. After that, you discovered that they weren't quite that frightening after all.

You may send that e-mail to the individual with whom you'd want to collaborate. Alternatively, you may phone the person you're interested in dating. Perhaps you hire a debt-reduction counselor and make a firm commitment to paying off your debt.

Here's an illustration:

If your aim is to own and operate a profitable six-figure firm, your priorities may include the following:

- Send everyone a copy of a newsletter

- Make a phone call to a lawyer to set up a limited liability company.

- Send an e-mail to a possible mentor who is currently engaged in the work I wish to pursue. This is a simple list of three little steps that, once taken, will make a significant effect. Learn to do this every morning when you wake up or immediately before you go to bed the night before, and then do it consistently!

- Find a partner who will hold you accountable.

• Accountability is a very crucial component of manifesting with ease. Your ability to manifest will increase in direct proportion to the number of positive and helpful individuals you surround yourself with who are also manifesting.

You may be experiencing difficulty following through on the manifestation tasks in this book at the moment. If you're feeling stuck, that's quite understandable. Having an accountability buddy will be beneficial. The purpose of having an accountability partner is to have someone with whom you can check in on a regular basis to assist keep you on track to achieving your goals. One of the most powerful motivators is the knowledge that you will have to inform someone whether or not you completed the task you said you would do. When you have an accountability buddy, you are far more likely to follow through on your plans. If no one else is aware of what you're up to, it's simple to come up with reasons why something didn't get done.

In addition to helping you stay on track, having an accountability partner provides you with a safe area in which to speak about your objectives, your next actions, and anything else that's holding you back from reaching your potential. If you run into difficulties, your accountability partner will be available to listen to you and provide you with encouraging words of support. Plus, it's usually simpler to realize your aspirations when you have a supportive community of individuals who are also striving to improve their own thinking.

When you initially start out in this arrangement, you may feel uneasy—especially if your spouse does not follow through on her promises. If she doesn't follow through, you might confront her with the question, "Why didn't you just do it?" Allow her the time and space she needs to come up with her own solution. Often, it is fear that prevents us from moving forward. It's possible that you're running out of time. Sometimes it turns out that what we thought we needed to accomplish wasn't all that vital after all, and that something else was more important after all. That's perfectly OK! It is your responsibility as a partner to gently keep the other person responsible, not by being cruel if your spouse does not follow through, but by asking her to reflect on her actions and feelings about them. Check to see whether she is still willing to commit to the activity and if so, establish a new deadline for when it will be completed.

You must remember that being too easy on each other would utterly destroy the point of the exercise. You'll discover that you and your partner motivate and encourage each other to take action, because when one of you starts to take steps toward your goals, the other feels the desire to keep up with the pace of the first. It's fantastic because it will inspire both of you to work harder. You may use your chats as a platform to share success stories and encourage one another to achieve their goals. The victories of one partner help to urge the other onward.

You're also there to provide moral support when you run into difficulties. You may even want to communicate more often or have a phone number available in case you get stuck and need assistance.

Once you start chatting, you'll be able to find out what method is the most effective for you.

How to put it in practice.

In order to actualize your goals, ask someone to serve as your accountability partner. They might be a member of your family, a friend, a coworker, or a fellow student. Writing down both your own and your accountability partner's aims is beneficial since you will have them as a reference for the following week when you check in. You may also send a copy of your list to your partner through email. Find out what works best for you and your partner.

Make a habit of doing something every day.

Every successful person I know has a daily routine that they follow. What is the first thing you do when you get up in the morning? Do you meditate, exercise, or prepare your breakfast? Do you schedule time each day for self-care activities? Have you increased your physical activity, prepared healthier meals, and participated in your favorite activity? I'm curious about your working hours. Do you only put in four hours a day at your job? If it seems implausible, believe me when I say that it isn't! Working hours are significant since they provide limitations for the amount of time that you are available to work.

You'll also have more concentration. The majority of individuals postpone and squander a significant amount of time. When you establish a time restriction for a project or work, you are essentially creating the expectation that you will have finished the project or task by that time. If you don't meet your time limit, the project or task will be abandoned.

Consider the following question: how would you want your day to look from the time you wake up in the morning to the moment you go to bed?

When it comes to developing a daily practice, time management is essential. When you wake up in the morning, you have a fresh chance to be your best self, to feel joy, and to generate wealth. Every day is a new beginning. After all, you don't materialize the things you wish to manifest. What you are manifests as what you are. The result is that your vibration will be raised if you're pleased and taking good care of yourself.

Currently, you have everyday behaviors that are merely a part of your daily life routine. You may utilize these habits to assist you in developing new routines that will help you achieve your big ambition. This may be accomplished by developing new rituals around them. They'll assist you in remaining organized and focused, particularly after you've cleared the clutter. What steps should you take to establish a ritualized routine? Start by incorporating a new ritual into an existing daily or weekly routine that you currently have. Adding a before or after to what you currently do might make this process more straightforward. Suppose you're ritualizing about tasks and you say something like:

- "After I have supper, I clean the dishes."

- "After I finish doing my laundry, I put my clothing away."

- My soiled clothing is placed in the washing machine after I take a shower.

- "As soon as I step in the door, I hang my keys on the key hook."

It seems to be easy, but it saves you a great deal of time when you are searching for items when you need them. You may also utilize these before-and-after statements to help you establish new manifestation techniques that will work for you. For example:

- "When I get up in the morning, I meditate."

- "After I meditate, I go to the gym for a half hour to work out."

- "While I'm eating breakfast, I'm watching a movie in my head."

- "I publish my priorities on my computer before checking my e-mail.

- "I publish my appreciation list on Facebook after I eat supper."

- "I go for a stroll in the fresh air before taking my lunch break."

The list may go on forever!

There shouldn't be any difficulty remembering these before and after statements. It seems to be so straightforward, yet the dishes may quickly pile up, and the neatly folded clothing might wind up resting on a table for many days rather than being returned to their proper place. Things don't become messy if you follow a set of procedures. You maintain your organization. You complete more tasks. You're happier and more liberated! It is quite vital to establish a regimen that you can stick to.

When you schedule time for exercise and other activities that you like, you'll feel better about yourself. You should also schedule dedicated time to concentrate on your major desire. Remember to take regular breaks and walk outdoors to get some fresh air on a daily basis as well. Spend as much time as you can in nature if at all feasible.

This will provide you with the emotional boost you need so that when you return to work on your ambition, you will be even more focused and motivated. Have you ever noticed that taking a break to attend your favorite yoga class or go for a run on the track outside allows you to get more work done in a shorter amount of time? This is due to the fact that taking time for self-care helps to improve mental clarity.

Your regular practice should be a non-negotiable part of your life. It is about making a promise to yourself that you will feel wonderful each and every day that you have a regular practice. As the day progresses, it's easy to get engrossed in the tasks you know you must do. However, if you begin your day by nourishing your soul, you will discover that you are in a better frame of mind to take action. Furthermore, if challenges arise that threaten to derail your plans, you will be better prepared to deal with them since you will have taken care of yourself first. Developing a daily routine is a genuine act of self-care.

How to Put it in practice.

Include in your manifestation notebook three rituals you may do on a daily basis to help center yourself and maintain a high vibrating state that will aid in your manifesting efforts. It might be anything as simple as meditating first thing in the morning, going for a run, or doing yoga. When you wake up, you may want to write down your dreams in a diary. Consider what makes you feel wonderful. Whatever it is for you, make a list of the everyday habits you want to adhere to in the future. Put your thoughts down on paper in the current time as a message to yourself. Consider the following scenario:

• When I wake up in the morning, I meditate before getting out of bed.

• After I clean my teeth, I write down my dreams in a diary.

• After that, I make a to-do list with just three items on it, and I check it twice.

Once you've established a regular practice, you'll begin to feel more in sync with the goals you've set for yourself.

Conquer your apprehension.

Your greatest talent is hidden behind your most terrifying dread. Given this knowledge, why wouldn't you want to do the thing that makes you the most nervous? Instead of focusing on what may happen if something goes wrong, consider what might happen if something goes well!

Remember anything from your history that you were terrified of doing at first but that eventually resulted in a great experience or reward if you're having trouble getting over your fear. You must have confidence in your abilities and believe that you are deserving of your ambitions. We're all good at coming up with excuses for why we can't accomplish something. You could believe that you don't know enough, or that you don't have the resources or money to get started. However, they are only justifications.

If you have an excuse, you won't have to accomplish anything and you won't be disappointed in yourself. If you are someone who procrastinates often, it is most likely due to a lack of motivation. You're terrified, so you keep putting off the one thing that you know would help you get closer to your goal. Even if you have no idea how anything is going to happen, all you have to do is ask for assistance.

Taking action is the most effective strategy to overcome fear. It is not necessary to have a lot of activity all at once. It might be as simple as taking a few steps every day.

Let me challenge you to face your fears and observe how you feel as a result of doing so. It's possible that you're afraid of:

- Sending an e-mail to a large number of people to solicit assistance

- Making the decision to pick up the phone and make the call you've been dreading.

- Making plans to attend that networking event

- Making an application for a new position.

- Creating your first blog post, and many more to come

It's important not to become too focused on the result. Maybe the universe has something even greater in store for you than you could have dreamed. So, keep your options open. It is not necessary for your activity to be flawless. If you wait until you have all of the information, you will never take action. Simply said, do what you can. Put yourself out there and have faith that you will learn and develop as a result of the experience. You will improve as you put in more hours of practice.

What's the worst that might happen in this situation? It's likely that you'll continue to reside in the same location as you do today. The question is, on the other hand, what is the greatest thing that may happen if you go through with your dream? I usually try to think about the best-case situation. As you can see, the bravery is in the act itself rather than in the result. It is through being vulnerable and putting yourself out there that you find success. Take pride in the fact that you completed the task in the first place.

How to Put it in practice.

Today, face a fear you've had for a long time. Despite the fact that it seems to be a simple exercise, it is really a strong releasing technique that will assist you in moving from being stuck to taking action. Remember, if you're frightened, envision things going nicely instead of negatively. Consider what you would want. Consider how you would feel if you could overcome any hurdle. What is the sensation like? Then you must take the necessary steps to overcome it.

Concentrate on your accomplishments rather than your failings. To overcome your hesitation to act, recall a moment in your life when you took a risk and the outcome was much better than you could have dreamed it would be. Consider what you've been able to achieve in your life as a result of your willingness to take action. The more your ability to see anything as an opportunity, the less fear you will experience. The cosmos is on your side, ready to assist you!

Your Dream Should Be Handled Like a Business.

Your vision must be taken more seriously now than ever before. If you want to demonstrate to the universe that you are serious about your ambition, you must approach it as if it were a legitimate company. Your dream, something you've been thinking about doing for a long time but haven't gotten around to accomplishing, is no longer on the back burner any more. Your dream is now the focal point of attention. It is your purpose, and it is your top priority.

A team of people and systems supporting you is required in order to bring your idea to fruition, and this includes your family and friends. In the case of a coffee shop, for example, you should seek the advice and assistance of other coffee shop owners before starting your venture. Try to find someone to serve as a mentor who has previously achieved the goals you want to achieve. You are not alone in feeling bewildered about how to go ahead with your efforts; don't be discouraged! All you need is some instruction from someone who has previously been there and done what you want to achieve in the past. The majority of successful individuals follow a model that was established by someone who has previously achieved success. As a result, you want to follow suit.

Once you've grasped the fundamental concepts, you may modify and recreate the model as necessary. However, you want to get some understanding of those who have gone before you.

I'm sure you're familiar with the adage that you must first understand the rules before you can violate them. Because of their vast experience and breadth of information, we seek to mentors for guidance and assistance. These people may assist you in being the person you want to be. There isn't any mystery behind it. We all need to seek guidance from persons who have a lot of knowledge in our industry. The thought of contacting someone you like may be intimidating at first. But, won't it feel great once your contact list is full with people you can call or email to ask for help? Don't you think it would be great to have some of the individuals you admire on your side?

A mentoring does not always have to be a long-term connection to be effective. A mentor might be as simple as someone with whom you talk on the phone to ask a few questions about how they got started in their career path. A book authored by someone who teaches you how to accomplish what you desire might serve as your mentorship source. Perhaps it's a memoir written by someone who has already achieved what you want to achieve.

I'm sure you recall what I said about overcoming your fears. This is the appropriate moment. We are all simply ordinary folks who have had comparable life experiences to one another. And we're all descended from the same wellspring. Instead of approaching your mentor as someone who is superior to you, treat him or her as a fellow human being and a friend. You are very remarkable! You have earned the privilege of being surrounded and supported by other wonderful individuals.

How to Put it in practice.

Start treating your desire like it is a company by first making a list of prospective mentors who might assist you in fulfilling your dream in your manifestation notebook. This is the first step in treating your dream like a business. Begin by thinking about five persons you admire. They might even be persons that are very well-known in their respective industries. That they possess some of the information you want to gain is vital to keep in mind. Try to locate the contact information for them or their helpers by doing some online research. Even if you are unable to locate their contact information, check to see if they are giving any public speeches, or if they have any performances or exhibits coming up that you would be interested in attending.

After that, make a list of another five possible mentors who are more approachable. Those present might be acquaintances or folks who live or work in the neighborhood.

Send Out a Few E-Mails.

Once you've identified these individuals, take the time to write them a couple e-mails in which you express your appreciation for their work and ask them to coffee or a phone chat in which you describe your current desire. Remember to keep the following suggestions in mind when you write your e-mails: Make a thorough investigation of the individuals. It's critical to acquire a sense of who they are and learn a little bit about their past before you get in contact with them. This demonstrates to them that you are really interested in them.

Give them a heartfelt thank you. Demonstrate to them that you are familiar with their professional or personal lives. People appreciate it when you take the effort to learn more about them and can demonstrate that you are aware of their accomplishments and challenges. If you know someone who knows someone they know, please sure to tell it to them! Because of this, the playing field will be leveled, and they will be more inclined to react. Inform them that you are interested in doing something similar to what they are doing (or have done) and that you would welcome the opportunity to ask them a few questions about how they arrived at their current position.

Keep the e-mail to a minimum. People who are busy do not like receiving lengthy e-mails. Make a point of following up. It is possible that they may not respond to you the first time. You'd be amazed at how enthusiastic a lot of individuals are about talking about their jobs and answering any questions you may have about how they got to where they are now. You never know, they could even be so interested in what you're working on that they want to provide a hand!

Do you have any questions?

When you finally get the opportunity to sit down with your possible mentor (which you will, since you are already working to make that meeting a reality), ask her or him the questions listed below:

• What path did you take to get to where you wanted to go?

- What were the first steps you took to get started?

- What was it like throughout the first few years of your career?

- Were there any errors you made that I should avoid doing in the future?

- To be successful in this industry or activity (or whatever your ambition encompasses), what talents do I need to possess?

- Is there anything I should be aware of in terms of resources?

Take notes while you're having a chat. You'll want to utilize these notes to guide you through the process of prioritizing your desire and developing action plans.

Network.

If you're visualizing a company, make a list of five industry events that you can attend in the next three months to network with other people. Make a note of these events in your calendar and make a point of attending at least one of them each month. When you go, be sure to:

Bring a stack of business cards with you. You want people to remember you and your accomplishments. The folks you meet will have a means to contact you as a result of this. Even better, approach other folks and ask for their business cards. This places you in a position of authority. You will be able to do the follow-up if you so want.

Wear something that will be remembered. I always want to wear a distinctive item, such as a jacket or a pair of shoes. It should be something that makes you feel good about yourself. Make contact with others and establish relationships. Finally, it's your turn to shine! Be true to yourself. Always be on the lookout for new information. Start with a series of questions. In most cases, if you inquire about someone's occupation, they will respond by asking you the same question back.

Follow up with the individuals you meet as soon as possible, while the memory of the encounter is still fresh in both your minds. You may do this by sending brief "Nice to meet you" e-mails to them, which can refresh their recollections of where you met and what you spoke about. Continue the discussion with them by phone or by meeting them for coffee if you choose. Tell them what it was about the talk that you enjoyed.

You will soar to greater heights if you find a mentor and surround yourself with successful individuals.

The moment you realize you are in the presence of greatness, you must rise to meet it. A certain technique to expedite the manifestation process is to do it this manner.

Create the squad of your dreams.

Once you've found a mentor, it's important to consider who else you can turn to for assistance so that you may devote your time and energy to realizing your ambition. If you're juggling too many tasks, it will be difficult to make significant progress on any one of them. "We should aspire to constantly be in our "zone of genius," which is the place in which our soul shines," says Gay Hendricks, the person who created the phrase "upper-limiting." If you're excellent at something, but someone else could easily do it for you, allowing you to spend more time doing what you genuinely like, it's time to delegate duties and chores to make your life simpler and more enjoyable. Similarly, if there are activities that you are presently doing that you are not enjoying at all, you will want to stop doing them immediately.

Consider who you would want to have on your team for each area and make a list of their names. Remember, you're putting down the assistance you want in your dream life, even if you have no idea how it will manifest itself at this time.

In the event that there is anything that you do not know how to do, or do not want to learn, you should employ someone to do it for you. Asking a buddy to assist you in a particular area is a good place to start. Alternatively, there are a large number of college students who would be delighted to work for you for free in return for real-world experience.

Once you've made the decision to seek assistance, you'll be able to locate the resources that will make it possible. With a solid support structure in place, you'll be less distracted by other duties, and you'll realize that you're able to manifest even more abundance as a result of having more time to devote to the things you like doing. Moreover, while you remain in a state of happiness, you draw the appropriate people and situations to you.

Make a list of daily reminders.

You should have a fairly decent concept of what your perfect life might look like by now, don't you? In addition, you've had some experience in stepping into it. However, barriers might appear that pull you out of a good state of mind that is conducive to manifesting. And it might be simple to lose sight of the fact that you are in the most ideal situation right now. While you're tending to your garden, it's a good idea to keep track of what you really planted! Gardeners sometimes erect signs in their gardens naming the vegetables they planted and include photographs of the finished produce to attract attention. It's not merely for the sake of being organized. You'll be less likely to pick out the sprouts before they've completely formed as a result of this method. And you recall that you've already sown seeds, and all that's left is for you to go on with the manifestation process as before. Your dreams will take time to manifest, so it's important to surround yourself with positive reminders of what you're working towards.

And if anything comes up that throws you off course and makes you question that your aspirations will come true, daily reminders will help you remain confident that everything is working out for your greatest benefit in the end. They may even educate your subconscious mind to tune into the frequency of the thing you're making, which is quite beneficial.

How to Put it in practice.

Make a habit of setting regular reminders to help you remember to remain focused on your long-term goals. Here are a few amusing suggestions:

• Changing your passwords for Facebook, your e-mail, and other programs you use on a regular basis to reflect one of your affirmations can help you stay on track. Use phrases such as "I earn

$350,000," "I am organized," or "Published Author" to describe your income.

• Create a note card with one of your affirmations written on it and stick it to your bathroom mirror so that you can see it every time you go to the restroom.

• Put up a poster depicting a scene from your ideal life (a house, a family, an awards event, or something similar) on the wall of your home. It might be a single photograph. Alternatively, you may make a vision board.

• As a bookmark for the book you're now reading, use one of the photos you selected or a note card with your affirmation written on it, as appropriate.

- Change the screen saver on your phone or computer to a representation of your perfect existence.

There are several approaches to creating daily reminders. Make the decision that seems right for you. There is no such thing as a good or incorrect answer, and you can never have too many reminders. You have a choice in everything, even this.

Make a schedule for your dreams.

This is something we've all done, but you're doing it purposefully this time, and you're committed to making your big goal a reality. So, if you haven't already, it's time to set a date for your big goal to come true.

What is the aim of putting the date on a calendar in the first place? Small steps add up to a big difference. As a result, when you put a date for the realization of your desire on your calendar, the universe begins to take your dream much more seriously. This is due to the fact that, on a subconscious level, you anticipate your dream manifesting on that day. You're also signaling to the world that you're making room for a new dream to take shape. Moreover, by scheduling your desire in your schedule, you're effectively saying no to everything else, creating a clear boundary that you're either manifesting your dream or something greater in its place.

In order to materialize your ideal home, for example, you should jot down the date on which you want to move in. Make a note of when you want to sell your existing residence, among other things. If you want to run a marathon, make a note of the day on which the event will take place. Once it's planned, you'll begin doing what you know you need to do to make it a reality as soon as possible.

How to Put it in practice.

Take a look at your calendar and mark the dates for your big ambition. I urge that you make use of a free online calendar. The fact that they're simple to alter and make it simple to organize recurring events means that you can plan events for years in advance. As soon as you've set the important dates, go back and schedule the minor tasks that will allow you to carry your goal ahead in the meantime.

Chapter Four

Using the Law of Attraction to Attract Love is a simple concept

In our lives, love is a vital component that we treasure in a number of ways that are beyond our abilities to comprehend them all. In our lists of wants and needs in life, we often rank love towards the top of the list, alongside other requirements such as health, housing, financial security, nutrition, and other necessities. Love is something that we all want on some level or another, and it may present itself in a number of different ways for different people. Everyone, including our family, friends, spouses, and even our neighbors and fellow citizens, wants to be loved by someone. When it comes to love and romance, these are things that make us feel fantastic on an emotional level, which is usually why we pursue them with such fervor.

Whenever it comes to manifesting the love life of your dreams, the law of attraction has the potential to be of immense assistance to you. You may find that the law of attraction may be of great aid to you, whether you desire to attract more love into your life, repair the love that is currently in your life, or otherwise work on your love life. Anybody who needs assistance with family, friends, spouses, or anybody else in their community will find it to be a fantastic resource. There are no constraints on who you may use the law of attraction to help you improve your relationship with, increasing the amount of love and affection that you feel for each other. There are no limitations on how you can use the law of attraction to help you improve your relationship. The law of attraction may be applied to anybody and anything. A range of situations, such as romantic love, platonic love, and the sort of basic admiration you have for others in your life, such as your coworkers or boss, may be taken advantage of by the law of attraction.

Here, we'll look at four incredibly important qualities of love that the great majority of people would want to see enhanced in their personal relationships. As we go forward, we will examine numerous strategies of attracting love, including finding your soul mate, persuading a boyfriend or girlfriend to propose to you, and even recovering power over an ex-boyfriend or girlfriend. Our talk will also cover themes such as familial ties and how you may either mend or just strengthen them in order for the love you feel to flow more freely in your life. A debate on friendships is also on the schedule, which will cover topics such as how to establish new friends and keep current ones, as well as how to restore friendships that have fallen on difficult times. The last topic is how to mend damaged relationships, including how to repair issues and arguments, endure difficult times, and generally heal love that has been hurt between you and others who are important to you.

Before we get into these specific areas of love, let's take a look at how you may improve the general quality of your relationship with the person you care about. Topics discussed include how to experience more love in a broad way, both between yourself and others as well as inside yourself. Listed below are some fundamental adjustments you may make to assist enhance your overall experience and the sensation of having more love in your life. Whether you want to experience and feel more love in your life or just want to live a life filled with more love and affection, there are some fundamental changes you can do to help enhance your overall experience and feeling of more love and affection. Here are some suggestions. The following six phases of affection practice will guide you through the process of building routines that will assist you in attracting more love into your life in general, in order to assist you in attracting more love into your life in particular.

To begin, you must first ask for the love that you want. Simply said, if you want to feel more love in your life, have better relationships, or give more freely of yourself, you should make a request of the universe to help you achieve your goals. Express yourself clearly and mention all of the parts of your love life that you would want to see improved in your request. The connections with friends, family, your spouse, acquaintances, colleagues, and your employment are all included in this category, as well as the relationships with oneself. Determine your course of action in a clear and concentrated manner, and make it a point to ask questions on a regular basis. In an ideal situation, you would enquire on a daily basis.

Believe in yourself and your ability to achieve success. We sometimes find it difficult to embrace the love we want into our lives because we think we are unworthy of such a connection, which is understandable. If you are having feelings of unworthiness or think that someone could not love you for any reason, it is critical that you begin to alter your beliefs in order for them to be more successful in serving your needs. To get rid of these limiting beliefs, you need to start focusing on the reasons why people can and should love you, rather than the reasons why they can't or shouldn't love you. Beginning to educate yourself on the fact that you, as well as everyone else, are worthy of love and acceptance is a good start. What matters is that you have made mistakes, been unkind to people in the past, or have qualities that you feel make you unlovable as a result of your upbringing or what others have said about you in the past. What matters is that you have had a painful breakup or a divorce, whether you have children or do not want children, or whatever else you are going through.

You are worthy of love exactly the way you are, regardless of your appearance. Every day, make a deliberate effort to believe what you've learned. If you want to realize this in yourself, you must first heal whatever wounds that may have happened in the past, and then you must face the reality that you are also deserving of love and acceptance. Your ability to accept and give unconditional love will get easier as you put more effort into mending and believing in yourself in the coming years.

Visualize yourself in a happy, satisfying relationship with the person you want to be your partner, and then write it down. Consider all of the ways that the love you give and receive will either enhance or negatively impact your life in some manner. Take the time to consider how much your life will alter as a consequence of your choice on a daily basis.

Can you imagine what it might feel like to be loved by someone else? In your opinion, how do you believe you'll be feeling? Do you have a vision for how you want your life to look? Having said that, do you intend to make any more phone calls in the near future? Do you intend to make more phone calls in the future? If so, how many? Do you want to spend more time with your family and friends, relishing their company and really appreciating their presence this holiday season? Will you start asking more fundamental questions on a regular basis, such as "how are you?" or "what's up?" If you react with a more direct and honest response, rather than a quick and curt "I'm OK" response that may or may not be truthful in the first place, what do you think will happen? When you're in a more vulnerable circumstance, what do you

159

imagine it will be like to be even more vulnerable? Write down all of the many ways that love will impact and improve your life, and then take the time to honestly assess how you will respond in each of these situations. If you realize that the response you are presently using has a tendency to block out love, you should consider choosing a different reaction from the one you are currently using. As an example, if you understand that someone loves you just the way you are and as a consequence, you stop returning their phone calls, picture what it would be like to pick up the phone and communicate with them more compassionately in line with the kind of relationship you have with this individual. On a daily basis, visualize how your life would be different in order to keep yourself motivated.

Adapt your behavior to that of a person with whom you are in a satisfying love relationship. Starting right now, if you want romantic love, begin acting in a way that invites love to enter your life immediately. Purchase a queen-size bed and sleep on one side of the bed so that you are prepared to share your bed with someone else if the situation warrants it. For example, if you currently live in a property that is more suited to a single person, you may want to consider getting a larger sofa or an additional seating arrangement for your home.

Make place in your bathroom or closet for someone who may use it in the near future by clearing out a drawer or two in your home. If you want to locate your pals, it is essential that you schedule time with them. Making new acquaintances should be a priority for you, so start by scheduling time on your schedule to do it. Even if you don't have any friends yet, you should start making some right away. Before meeting new people, spend your time communicating with family and friends, visiting areas where you could meet new people, or just imagining what your life would be like after meeting new people. Being present in the present allows you to open your time and your heart in order to accept the love that you seek via your actions.

Receive the love that you so much want. That's when the fruits of your religious beliefs and therapeutic activities will begin to show themselves in your life. The most important thing to remember as love starts to find its way into your life is to be open to accepting it. Avoid being scared and enabling outmoded ideas and habits to take root in your mind, which will lead you to believe that you are inadequate and that others are undeserving of your affection. The ability to create distance and push them away in order to not have to be as near to them is not a good tactic to use in this situation. You should instead devote your efforts to building genuine and rewarding relationships with other individuals. Put up the same amount of effort into your relationship as you would expect the other person to put forward. Alternatively, if it turns out that they are not the right person for you and the relationship ends as a consequence, take advantage of this excellent opportunity to learn how to stay open to meeting the correct person the next time around. Make sure you don't use that as justification for isolating yourself and convincing yourself that you are genuinely unworthy of love.

Even if you succeed, your efforts will be fruitless, and you will swiftly reverse whatever progress you have made toward your objectives.

As you are well aware, thankfulness is a fundamental component of the practice at all times, as you have seen. When it comes to expressing your gratitude to someone close to you, there are a variety of good and inventive ways to go about it. Communicate to the people in your life that you really care about them, that you appreciate their friendship, and that you like having them around. Provide opportunities for the people you care about to know how much they mean to you, and do not be afraid to tell them on a regular basis. You should never be reluctant to share your thoughts about an argument or a falling out with someone, or to attempt to repair the relationship if you think it is appropriate to do so. It's important to remember that everyone has a disagreement at some point in their life. Following the conclusion of this section, you will learn about the many techniques that may be utilized to settle these disputes in a way that is honorable and courteous to all parties involved. Whenever the opportunity presents itself, show your gratitude to those who have helped you, and never be afraid to convey your feelings to others in a straightforward and honest way. Regarding romantic and non-romantic relationships, the appreciation of the other person may be discovered in their vulnerability toward the other person.

Numerous people realize that they are having problems attracting love as a result of a variety of life circumstances and a suitcase full of psychological baggage. Often, rather than the other person, we are the ones who are at the root of the problem. We are not in the counseling profession, and this book is not designed to aid you in sifting through your baggage or your history, yet it is important to understand when it comes to attracting love. It is essential that you have a high degree of self-awareness when it comes to utilizing the law of attraction and combining the six phases of attraction into your love-attracting activities in order to be successful.

Investing substantial time and attention into two crucial processes can help us attract love more effectively: believing and receiving. Several studies have shown that many people reject love because they believe they do not deserve it, and as a consequence, they close themselves off to the prospect of receiving it. Both of these limiting beliefs are directly responsible for our incapacity to receive, and both of these issues contribute to our inability to attract the love we desire to ourselves. To be effective in attracting the love you want, you must commit a large amount of time and attention to these two aspects of the procedure. You will be able to effortlessly attract love into your life if you are effective at adjusting your thinking and opening yourself up to receive without restriction and limitations. Love may be found almost everywhere. Although you may not be aware of it at the time, it's literally all around you at this very now. The presence of love can be found everywhere, whether it is love that is given to you by someone else, love that is given to someone else by someone else, or even love that is given to yourself by yourself. Love can be found in all forms. No matter how alone we may feel in a room with no one to talk to, there is never a time when love does not exist in our hearts and minds. It doesn't matter whether you realize it or not, the limiting beliefs you have established to protect yourself from love are a kind of self-love, even if they exist in a toxic manner by preventing love from entering your life. In a different way of looking at it, love is something that exists for you, by you, and exists to protect you from being damaged in any way. The kind of love that is deep and sincere, but it is also the kind of love that has the ability to keep other true loves away. We will work on improving this in combination with the six steps of the attraction process in order for you to be able to activate the law of attraction and attract the love of anyone you choose to yourself.

Anyone who want to increase the amount of love in their life should participate in this activity. It is possible to attract a new relationship, get a proposal from your present spouse, increase the quantity of love you receive from your current partner, make new acquaintances, or generally attract love into your life by practicing the following techniques.

Following is a description of how it works:

People who are drawn to this specific kind of attraction account for a small proportion of the population. We were drawing external items from an external point of view in our previous law of attraction operations, and this is still the case in our current efforts. Obtaining funding from a third-party source is an example of such an endeavor. However, for this specific session, we shall be confined within the building. We will attract a more wholesome and open environment that is open and ready to receive the love that we seek to attract from those from whom we wish to attract it, and we will do it in a more wholesome and open way than we have previously experienced. You should pay close attention to this kind of internal attraction because it will be quite advantageous when it comes to attracting love into your life via the law of attraction.

When it comes to getting what you want, the first step is generally to communicate your desire for it. "How can I open myself up so that I may attract the love that I desire?" is a question that you might want to consider asking yourself in this circumstance. The vast majority of the time, people are utterly unaware of what it is inside themselves that causes them to close themselves off to love.

When it comes to discovering the root of the problem, we will work with you to alter your viewpoint and move beyond it, so effectively opening yourself up to attract the love you desire once again.

Following that, you must believe that it is a realistic goal. While you may not know how to alter your ideas in order to correct the thinking at this time, you want to have faith that you will be able to do so once you understand why this is occurring. Also, you want to believe that you are capable of identifying the underlying reason in the first place, and that you will be able to effortlessly attract the person or results that you want as a result of doing so in the subsequent phases. As soon as you have the circumstances that you want, whether it is a new spouse, a proposal, or anything else, you should concentrate on extending your views in order to properly embrace that situation. In a subsequent section, we'll explain more about the assignment's receiving component.

In addition to reinforcing your beliefs, visualization may improve your ability to uncover the answer to how you can open yourself up and heal any obstructions that may be present in your life. Concentrating on what your life will be like when you have been able to properly welcome the love you desire into your life via visualization is a fantastic way to strengthen your attention and focus on what you want. Given that love is something that virtually everyone wishes they had more of in their lives, it is likely that you have spent a great deal of time thinking about what your life would be like if you were more open to it. Work with those thoughts and put your heart and soul into them, acknowledging all of the ways in which this new level of love may improve and benefit your life as you go about your day to day activities.

After you have spent time picturing your perfect relationship, you should begin acting in line with your intentions for attracting love. Take note of any actions that the imaged version of yourself took differently, and then begin to mimic those actions. Practice being more vulnerable, speaking out more, stepping out of your comfort zone, and allowing as much love into your life as you possibly can. Practice being more vulnerable. Begin with little acts of kindness, such as someone holding the door open for you or giving you a hug whenever you need one, then work your way up to larger and larger gestures of generosity. As you get more used to it, you may find yourself welcoming love into your life in bigger and more evident expressions than before. When you reach a certain point in your development, you will be able to accept love freely and effectively, just as your envisioned version of yourself has done so.

Following that comes the receiving stage, which, as you are well known, is a crucial phase in the process of attracting love into your life. After that comes the giving stage. When love comes your way, you must be open to receive it, no matter how unexpectedly it arrives. It is critical that you do not isolate yourself, close yourself off, or otherwise make yourself unreceptive to the love you have asked for in this situation. Consider taking advantage of this opportunity to evaluate your ideas and assess whether or not they need to be updated in order for you to freely receive the love you desire and feel worthy of it at the same time.

Finally, express your gratitude for the love that has been pulled into your life so far by your actions. In the event that you have found someone new, make it a point to explain to them how much you appreciate them and how grateful you are to have them in your life as soon as possible. As soon as you have been asked to marry someone, show your thanks to them by saying that you are grateful that they chose you to be their partner and that you are grateful that they asked you to spend the rest of your life with them. Be mindful of the fact that, if you have seen a big rise in your spouse's affection for you, you should express your appreciation to them for acting in this way toward you and express your thanks for them behaving in this manner toward you. Those who recognize that you value them and their business are significantly more likely to remain with you for the long run.

The following are the stages involved in a meditation for attracting love:

For the purpose of this meditation, we shall focus on welcoming love into our daily life. In this two-part meditation, you will discover how to both open yourself up and attract the love that you want. In order to accommodate this, the meditation will be little longer than normal this time. Thank you for taking the time to sit or lie down in a comfortable position where you will be undisturbed for many minutes. Please make sure that all of your comfort requirements have been met so that you do not get distracted while listening to the presentation. Please use the restroom, drink some water, and, if you feel the need, lay down with a blanket on the floor. Please take a few moments to unwind. As soon as you are ready, you may begin the meditation session in full.

You should take a deep breath and relax at your current place right now, if that's OK with you. Feel the support that your body is receiving from the surface on which you are sitting, and express your thanks. Make yourself comfy in your chair or bed and close your eyes for a moment. If you are conscious of how peaceful it is for you to be here, I want you to focus on being open to feeling this calmness as often as possible. It's astonishing how quickly and effortlessly it comes to you right now. It seems as if you could stay in this posture for hours on end as your breathing grows deeper and softer as you sink further into this state of relaxation. Aside from the physical relaxation that results from your activities, you also become conscious of the mental relaxation that has occurred. Your guard gradually comes down, allowing this sense of peace and satisfaction to pour over you and into your being at this very now.

When you're ready, I want you to see yourself standing in a meadow somewhere, and then tell me about your experience. Obviously, you are able to personalize the meadow as you like. For example, you may choose to include trees or flowers in your meadow as well as a creek flowing through it as the background to your design. Your meadow may be alive with butterflies that flutter around, or it may be full with little bunnies that bounce about. You can find yourself the only one in the room, as an alternative. Your meadow may be visualized in any way you wish it to be, as well as in whichever way seems to be the most peaceful to you at that particular time. I want you to imagine yourself laying down on the ground with your back against the grass when you are finished when you are ready. Please lie down with your legs out straight and your arms spread out to the sides, palms facing up, as though you were ready to receive blessings from the cosmos. In your sleep, I want you to be conscious of a magnificent, dazzling white light that is now filling your heart region and that you should be aware of it. This white light may seem dull at first, or it may be vivid and flaming straight away when it first turns on, depending on the manufacturer. This light is completely up to you in terms of how you choose to welcome it into your heart. Once you've done so, though, I want you to visualize a lovely white light beaming into your heart, enabling it to grow. This is what I mean by "letting your heart to expand." As it starts to glow, you may notice that your heart begins to open. You will be able to feel your love flowing freely once more since the white light will wipe away whatever obstacles you may be feeling. The more you open your heart and mind to yourself and your surroundings, the more you will notice that you are freely loving yourself and your surroundings, as well as embracing the love that you are receiving from yourself, your surroundings, and this beautiful white light. Finally, when you are ready, you may think that the sun is rising and that the light is beginning to shine upward. As a result, a chord begins to form, which reaches from your heart space out into the world outside yourself. Once this is completed, it will continue to fly out into space, reaching out to the specific people that you choose. Despite your best attempts, the chord continues to grow longer and longer, reaching as far as it has to in order to reach the person whose love you so much want to be with you. As the wire becomes longer, it does not get thinner, more stretched, or duller in appearance. Instead, it retains its tensile strength, luminous brilliance, and dimensional stability. It makes unhindered progress in the direction of the person whose adoration you yearn for until it comes across them. After that, it develops a link with their heart's central nervous system. As a consequence of this, you may experience an increase in feelings of love inside you. Nothing can stop it from flowing freely between the two of you. There are no boundaries between you. Absolutely nothing can hold the love at bay, and absolutely nothing can prevent it from developing. Your fondness for one another seems to be mutual, and you appear to be getting affection from one another. After you've had a chance to bask in the love for a few moments, I want you to imagine the wire gradually becoming invisible to you as it slowly disappears. It will remain as a constant reminder in the back of both of your thoughts as you both prepare to love one another openly and freely on a whole new level of closeness. As soon as you are ready, I want you to gently bring your attention back to yourself in the meadow where you are now standing. There you are, soaking in the love that has been freely given to you by the person from whom you had hoped to receive it in the first place. It is a beautiful thing. Once your awareness has returned to the present moment, you may bring it back to the present moment by being aware of the space in front of your eyes. Open your eyes slowly and gently, bringing your attention back to the current instant in time. When you get back, take note of how different you feel as a consequence of your openness to offer and accept love in return. It is OK to continue this meditation as many times as you like in order to feel as if you are ready to freely accept and receive the love that you desire."

Relationships within a family.

Not only do sexual relationships exist, but so does a general love of humanity. In fact, it may be seen in many family relationships as well as social situations. If you want to improve the amount of love that you experience in your family relationships, the law of attraction may be able to provide you a considerable advantage in terms of reaching achievement. You must first allow yourself to be open to obtaining a more positive relationship with your family before you can expect to receive one. The law of attraction may also be of use in repairing relationships that have been damaged in the past. It may also be possible to use a similar method to help you get closer to members of your family who you like but with whom you have not felt particularly connected in the past, such as cousins or other distant relatives.

This meditation is aimed for everyone who want to strengthen their family relationships and make them more permanent in their life in some way. The law of attraction may assist you in achieving your objectives, whether you want to increase the quantity of love in an existing relationship or heal a broken relationship so that the flow of love can resume. With the aid of the law of attraction, it is possible to bring families back together and to strengthen the love that they have for one another in a straightforward way, with no effort.

Following is a description of how it works: Navigating family relationships may be tough. The art of attracting love is often centered on attracting a space inside ourselves that is open to receiving love. However, love in family relationships frequently involves us maintaining space for healing while still being open to receiving the love we desire. Sometimes the process may need us to reframe the love we get, while other times it will include us receiving exactly what we want. Depending on the situation, the law of attraction component might be simple or quite complex. If you want to put it another way, the law itself is straightforward: it will help you to assist any healing that you may need, to hold space for yourself as well as for your family members, and to learn how to embrace the love you desire from those closest to you. The six-step approach that follows will instruct you on how to make optimal use of this instrument in your business.

Conclusion

The law of attraction is a fundamental idea that applies to all aspects of life. When it comes to global society, this universal norm describes how we should behave ourselves while also outlining what we should expect in return. When it comes to manifesting our desires, the law of attraction says that we should anticipate what we want rather than just asking for what we want. When we ask for anything, the universe is eager to provide us with what we seek. Consider this: when a flower needs sunlight, it is provided with it. Dirt is found when a tree need it in order to bury its roots in the ground. When a pregnant wolf is ready to give birth, she may enter a cave to give birth. Every time a living organism in our universe need anything to further its existence and the life of the universe, the resources necessary to do this are made immediately accessible to it. Consider if it would be naïve and selfish of you to believe that you are the only living person on the face of the planet who is undeserving of the resources necessary to survive. If you believe this, consider the following: Yes, it would be considered disrespectful in my opinion. The universe did not create and nurture you into your present condition just for the purpose of depriving you of everything you need to live. In its place, it is actively prepared to provide you with anything you need, want, or want in order for you to not only progress in life, but also enjoy it to the fullest degree that is reasonably feasible.

The universal life force energy yearns to be awakened and experience life. Because you are a life, you are the body through which a life receives the opportunity to have its experiences. It is inevitable that those who refuse to embrace and appreciate their experiences will eventually perish and fade away. It is primarily your job to mobilize all of the resources you need in order to live your life to the fullest degree possible, in whatever way you see fit. The universe gains the opportunity to hope that it will be able to experience its one true love: life as a result of your actions.

The vast majority of people are completely unaware that they have already mastered the law of attraction, which is a common misconception. Pain and bad health have become the focus of their existence, as they are focused with how much their bodies hurt and how terrible their health has become. Their bodies do not seem to be the way they would want them to be, and they often feel as if they are in a state of chaos and ruin as a result. They are preoccupied with how little money they have and how tough it is for them to pay their bills; as a result, less money comes in and the battle becomes more intense. They are obsessed with how little love they have in their lives, or with all of the ways love has failed them and continues to fail them, and as a consequence, they are unable to experience love in their own lives. The more they focus on how routine, dull, or unpleasant their lives are, the more banal, boring, and unappealing their lives become as a consequence of their efforts. But here's the thing: you're the only one who suffers and fails as a result of your self-destructive ideas and obsessions. No one else is affected. Due to the fact that it is experiencing life in one of its many manifestations, the universe is not in agony. If it desires, it will go through whatever forms life takes on and you have chosen to be the vessel through which it does so in a life filled with pain, agony, and death for its own amusement.

You have complete influence over the co-creation of your own existence, thanks to the hand of the universe. Choose where you direct your focus, what you give your attention to, and what you let into your life. You have the capacity to make these decisions. The decisions you make about your one-of-a-kind existence are totally up to you. The universe will always be more than happy to provide you with anything you need in order for you to continue living life to the maximum extent possible. The only choice you have to make is whether you want to assist the universe in experiencing its most awful experiences through you, or whether you want to assist the universe in experiencing its most amazing experiences through you. Neither option is undesirable.

It is inside the pages of this book that you will find every single key criterion you will need to acquire the art of the law of attraction. You've had the opportunity to think about the six fundamental phases of the process, how you might apply them in a variety of situations to help you optimize your life experiences and improve your overall quality of life, and how you might increase your positive energy as a result of these considerations. Throughout this course, you'll have the option of listening to over twenty wonderful meditations that will each aid you in understanding the law of attraction and enabling the utmost degree of attraction attainable in your life, which is limitless. The law of attraction is also explained in detail, as is the way that you could naturally reject it. You've also learned how to fight these natural tendencies so that you can reap the full advantages of your efforts. It is now just necessary for you to act on a regular basis and to accept all of the gifts that have been presented to you so far.

Made in the USA
Middletown, DE
21 May 2022